ESSENTIAL GUIDE TO TREAT DIABETES AND TO LOWER CHOLESTEROL

ESSENTIAL GUIDE TO TREAT DIABETES AND TO LOWER CHOLESTEROL

Treat (Pre)diabetes and **Lower Cholesterol**

HOWARD T. JOE, M.S., PH.D.

ISBN: 979-890181-069-9

Essential Guide to Treat Diabetes and to Lower Cholesterol
Copyright © 2012 by Howard T. Joe, M.S., Ph.D

Yorkshire Publishing
3207 South Norwood Avenue
Tulsa, Oklahoma 74135
www.YorkshirePublishing.com
918.394.2665

CONTENTS

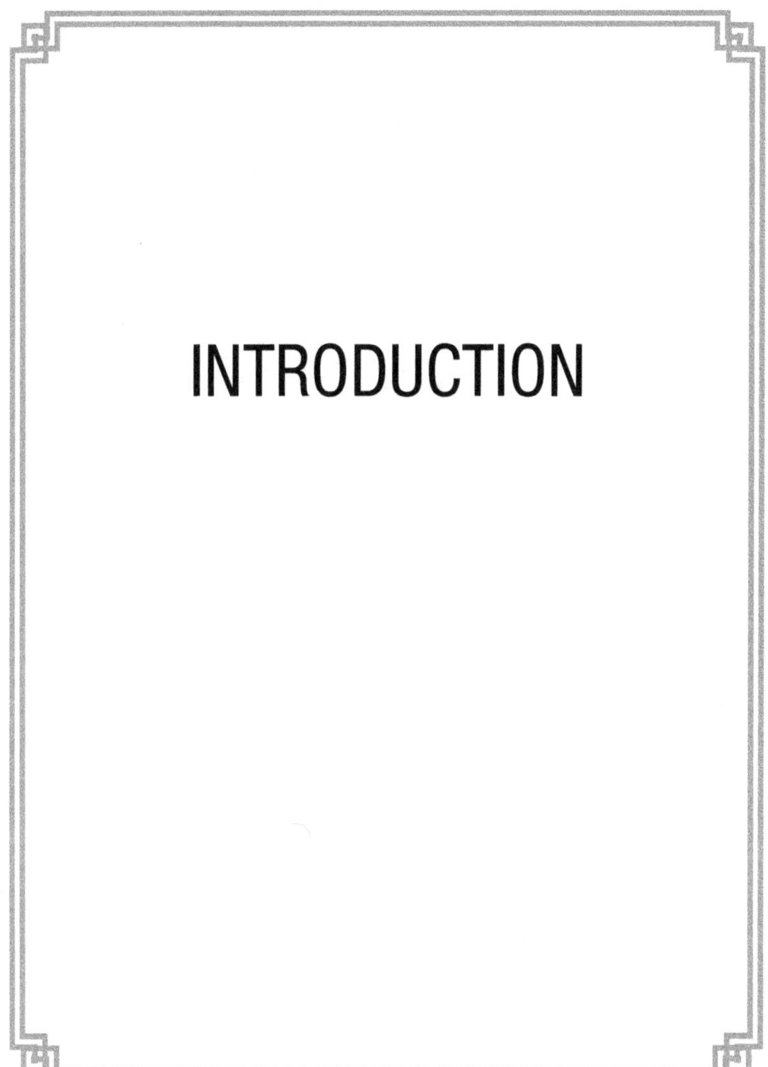# INTRODUCTION

Diabetes is a serious disease.[1] It affects more than 25 million people in the U.S. and about 180 million people worldwide. The serious effects associated with this disease include heart attack, stroke, kidney damage, lost arm or leg, nerve damage, and eyesight blindness.[1] It was even reported that diabetes is the leading cause of new cases of blindness in adults in the United States.[2] Clearly, a very effective method is needed to treat the harmful effects of diabetes, and this book provides such method.

Author Howard T. Joe was a pre-diabetic. By using the method described in the book, however, he has been able to lower his fasting blood glucose to 90s and 100s without using medication. Furthermore, using this book's method has also lowered a few of his diabetic relatives' fasting blood glucose from about 170 to 100s/110s. This was accomplished through a treatment that included taking Metformin ER and/or other medication and common natural foods as described in the book. In essence, the book's method has been tested and verified with a limited number of people. Moreover, the book's method is a natural and healthy method with common natural foods and with references to support their effectiveness.

Besides the benefit of reducing blood glucose, an additional advantage for taking soluble fiber is lowered total blood cholesterol.[4] Joe's total fasting blood cholesterol was in the 210s range. But by using this book's method, he has been able to lower his fasting total blood cholesterol to 159 and 160s without taking cholesterol lowering medication.

Since the author was able to obtain good, healthy results by using the book's method, readers can likewise hope to achieve similar results by following the book's method. The next chapter deals with the importance of having a physical checkup that includes a fasting blood test. It is followed by a section on soluble fiber that lowers blood glucose and reduces total cholesterol. In this section, common natural foods that contain soluble fibers are discussed. The next chapter reviews common natural foods that contain magnesium to lower blood glucose. Finally, the last section deals with a complete recipe to lower blood glucose and total cholesterol.

PHYSICAL CHECKUP

As obesity increases in population, type 2 diabetes becomes more common. Coupled with new cases of type 1 diabetes, the total number of diabetic cases increases daily. Obviously, the first step to treat pre-diabetes and diabetes is to have a physical checkup. After an examination, the physician may prescribe a medication. A good medication for type 2 diabetes to start is Metformin in the extended release form (ER). Generally, a patient takes Metformin ER and/or other medication in the morning and another Metformin ER after supper. Metformin ER is a generic pill that requires a doctor's prescription. It lowers blood glucose levels by blocking the liver's release of glucose and reducing its resistance to insulin.

As part of the physical checkup, a fasting blood glucose is needed to determine whether a person is pre-diabetic or diabetic. A normal fasting blood glucose level is less than 100 mg/dL. A fasting blood glucose level at or above 126 mg/dL indicates diabetes. If the first test result shows a person is diabetic, then a second test is needed to confirm the result. In addition, the fasting blood test also gives the cholesterol levels.

SOLUBLE FIBER LOWERS BLOOD GLUCOSE AND TOTAL CHOLESTEROL

Since plant foods contain soluble fibers and/or insoluble fibers, it is important to select the right plant foods. There are two kinds of soluble fiber sources. One type is from food sources, and the other kind is the supplemental source. It has been reported that water-soluble fiber helps to regulate blood sugar.[3] It also has been reported that soluble fiber lowers cholesterol.[4]

The following vegetables and fruits contain soluble fiber: oats, barley, beans, eggplant, okra, soybeans, apples, and strawberries.[4] Barley, which contains gluten, decreases blood sugar by reducing the sugars from food.[5] Having barley at breakfast, barley soup at lunch, and barley at supper can lower the fasting blood glucose by 20 to 30 points overnight. It was reported that apples, which contain soluble fiber called pectin, lower blood glucose, as pectin helps to slow down how fast glucose can enter the bloodstream.[6] As barley decreases blood glucose, rice and potatoes, however, increase blood glucose.[7] A good replacement for rice and potatoes is sugar-free bread.

Spinach, kale, cabbage, chickpeas, eggplant, okra, and soybeans are good vegetables that contribute little to blood glucose increase. In fact, okra, eggplant, soybeans, and chickpeas also contain soluble fiber that can lower blood glucose.[3] These vegetable soluble fibers have an additional advantage by combining with insoluble fibers to fulfill the daily fiber requirement.

MAGNESIUM DECREASES BLOOD GLUCOSE

It was reported that magnesium helps to regulate blood sugar levels, which decreases blood glucose.[8] Thus, magnesium can lower the fasting blood glucose of both pre-diabetes and diabetes. Flax and sesame seeds are a great source of heart healthy oils and also provide a good source of magnesium. For example, there are 39 milligrams of magnesium per tablespoon of flaxseeds.[9] Thus, taking two tablespoons of flaxseeds daily provides almost twenty percent of the daily magnesium requirement. Since flaxseeds are usually grounded powder, it can be easily added to food sources.

Avocado is another great source of magnesium. For example, there are 70 milligrams of magnesium in one medium avocado.[10] Avocado also has a good source of omega 3 fatty acids that are good for general health. Spinach and kale also contain magnesium, as do walnuts, sunflower seeds, and pumpkin seeds.[10] In addition, tofu (which is made from soybean, calcium sulfate, and magnesium chloride) provides 37 milligrams of magnesium per 100 grams of tofu.[11] It is important to have enough magnesium because it was reported that people who have type 2 diabetes often have low levels of magnesium in the blood.[12]

RECIPE TO LOWER BLOOD GLUCOSE AND TOTAL CHOLESTEROL

A good recipe for lowering the fasting blood glucose from about 170 to 100s/110s for type 2 diabetes is to take Metformin ER and/or other medication in the morning and to take another Metformin ER after supper. Along with taking Metformin ER and/or other medication in the morning, have an oatmeal breakfast and add two tablespoons of flaxseed to obtain magnesium and heart healthy omega 3 fatty acids. Next, take barley soup at lunch. Barley soup is available in nearly any supermarket. At supper, take barley and sugar free bread with meat or fish along with eggplant and chickpeas or other vegetables like soybean, spinach, kale, or cabbage. Finally, take Metformin ER after supper.

Good daily fruit sources that maintain low blood glucose levels are apples and avocados. Since apples contain pectin-soluble fiber and avocados contain magnesium, they can also help to lower blood glucose. To complete a healthy and natural recipe for good health, it is important to consume nuts and seeds like walnuts, sunflower seeds, and pumpkin seeds, which also contain magnesium to lower blood glucose. It is mainly the soluble fiber and magnesium that lowered the author's fasting pre-diabetes blood glucose to 90s and 100s without taking medication.

The above described common natural food method has a supplementary, additional advantage: lowering the author's fasting total cholesterol from about 210s to 159 and 160s without taking medication. It is mainly the soluble fiber in the common natural foods that lower the cholesterol.

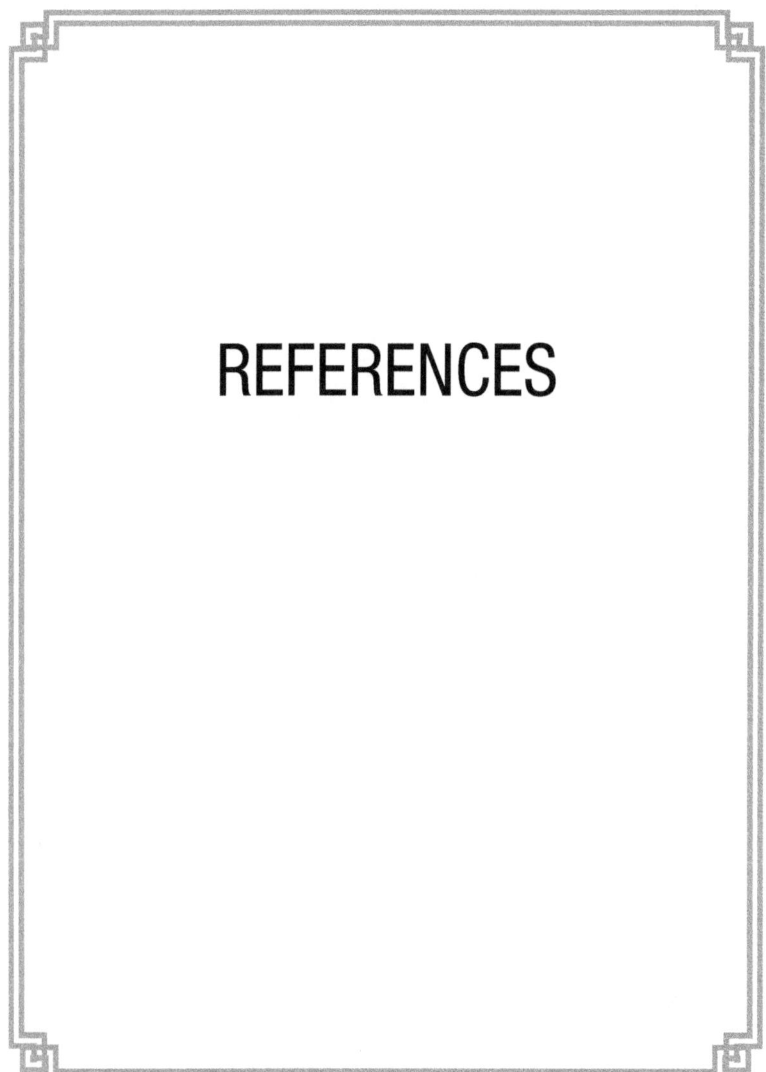

REFERENCES

Introduction

1. WebMD, "The Risks and Complications of Uncontrolled Diabetes." http://diabetes.webmd.com/risks-complications-uncontrolled-diabetes.

2. Wiegman, Stacy. "How can poor control of my diabetes harm my health?" (online forum message). sharecare. http://www.sharecare.com/question/poor-control-diabetes-harm-health.

Soluble Fiber Lowers Blood Glucose and Total Cholesterol

3. SparkPeople., "Figuring Out the Facts on Fiber." http://sparkpeople.com/resource/reference_fiber.asp.

4. Harvard Heart Letter. 20. no. 2. October (2009).

5. WebMD, "Barley: Uses, Side Effects, Interactions and Warnings." http://www.webmd.com/vitamins-supplements/ingredientmono-799-BARLEY.aspx?activeIngredientId=799&activeIngredientName=Barley.

6. Cee, Jenna. LiveStrong.com, "Fruits & Vegetables to Control Blood Sugar

Levels." http://www.livestrong.com/article/436165-fruits-vegetables-to-control-blood-sugar-levels/.

7. wise GEEK, "How Can I Lower My Blood Sugar?" http://www.wisegeek.com/how-can-i-lower-my-blood-sugar.htm.

Magnesium Decreases Blood Glucose

8. Office of Dietary Supplements, "Magnesium–Health Professional Fact Sheet." http://ods.od.nih.gov/factsheets/Magnesium-HealthProfessional/.

9. Healthaliciousness, "Top 10 Foods Highest in Magnesium." http://www.healthaliciousness.com/articles/foods-high-in-magnesium.php.

10. Dallas-Fort Worth Vegetarian Education Network, "Magnesium, Mg, Content of Foods." http://dfwnetmall. com/veg/magnesium-content-foods. htm.

11. Diet & Fitness Today, "Magnesium in tofu."http://www.dietandfitnesstoday. com/magnesium-in-tofu.php.

12. University of Maryland Medical Center, "Magnesium." http:// www.umm.edu/altmed/articles/ magnesium-000313.htm.

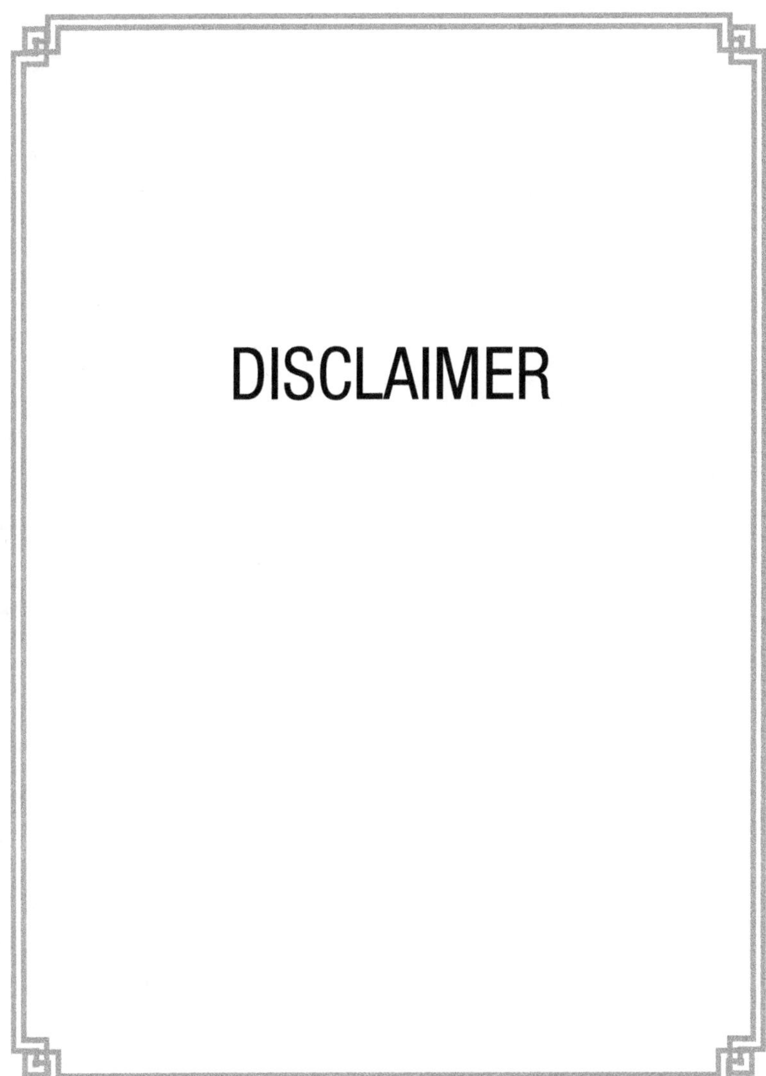

DISCLAIMER

The information in this book is not intended or implied to be a substitute for professional medical advice, diagnosis or treatment. All material in this book is for general information purposes only. The author and publisher make no representation and assume no responsibility for the accuracy of information contained in this book and such information is subject to change without notice. You are encouraged to confirm any information obtained from or through this book with other sources, and review all information regarding any medical condition or treatment with your physician. NEVER DISREGARD PROFESSIONAL MEDICAL ADVICE OR DELAY SEEKING MEDICAL TREATMENT BECAUSE

OF SOMETHING YOU HAVE READ IN THIS BOOK.

The author and publisher do not recommend, endorse or make any representation about the efficacy, appropriateness or suitability of any specific tests, products, procedures, treatments, services, opinions, or other information that may be contained in this book. THE AUTHOR AND PUBLISHER ARE NOT RESPONSIBLE NOR LIABLE FOR ANY ADVICE, COURSE OF TREATMENT, DIAGNOSIS OR ANY OTHER INFORMATION, SERVICES OR PRODUCTS THAT YOU OBTAIN IN CONNECTION WITH THIS BOOK.